REDEEM

NOT TOO BIG TO WEEP

a poetry anthology

STEVE PAGE

First Printing: 2017

ISBN: 9781549894701

DEDICATION

This book is dedicated to my mother,
Joan Page.

Contents

ACKNOWLEDGEMENTS

You wouldn't be reading this collection of poems without some key catalysts.

First, thanks to the likes of David Kossoff and Steve Turner, whose writing excited me many years ago. I would also like to thank The Poetry School and Tamar Yoseloff for giving my writing a firm foundation.

My poems were first taken out of my desk drawer because of an opportunity offered by PROOST.CO.UK, when they brought together their anthology, Learning to Love (curated by Chris Goan).

I encourage you to seek out the poems and writings from each of these writers.

I owe so much thanks to many friends and family along the way that I can't fit in here. You and I know who you are.

And I'd like to voice a big thank you to Pete Cornford and the family at Redeemer London for their hugs, laughs, encouragement and opportunities to read my poetry out loud to a discerning audience.

Lastly, thank you to Sam Isaacson, whose wise words and friendship have helped bring this book together. He also puts together a cool book cover design.

It may take a village to raise a child but it took many more to get me here.

I was tempted to voice thanks to God here. But my love and gratitude to God the Father, God the Son and God the Holy Spirit is better expressed in my poetry.

So read on.

FOREWORD

Steve Page is one of the most wonderful people I have had the privilege of meeting. He is baffling in his capacity to look after people, to champion friends when they're down and to give what are indisputably the best hugs ever given.

Steve is also an incredible example of what it means to be a man. He is a father to many more than just his biological children, he has a powerful strength of will and character, but he is also utterly transparent and bold in his display of emotions. He cries when he is moved and is (refreshingly) unapologetic about it, and he is full of empathy for others.

I can think of no better compliment for this collection of poems than to say that my friend Steve comes through beautifully page after page; reading it is moving, inspiring and chuckle-inducing.

I couldn't recommend it more.

Yvette Flower

Introduction

How many poets does it take to change a light bulb?

Two - One to hold the ladder, and one to tearfully consider the transitive nature of existence compounded by the tragedy of the assumption of replacement without true celebration of the individuality found at the heart of the mass produced and the beauty that can be found in a frail light fighting against the darkness inherent in an unfair world.

I'm not sure what comes to mind at the thought of a poet or poetry; perhaps wordy antiquated language, perhaps someone with their head in the clouds. The greatest compliment I received about my poetry was from someone at church. We were chatting about poetry and she said, "I'm not a great one for poetry. I can never figure out what they're on about. Oh, I don't mean your poems, Steve, I understand yours."

We can't all be Keats. The poems you'll discover between these pages wouldn't win any literary prizes. But they are my attempt at conveying my experience of life with a smile on my face. Some are clearly born from my walk with Jesus. Some are just daft. Some are both. Whether you share my faith or not, I hope you'll find them entertaining and some-times thought provoking.

From Godzilla to samosas. From psalms to 70's rock. Each poem reflects a bit of me.

I've split the poems up into themes to make it a little easier to find your way around. Some could have been included under more than one theme, but most were easy to allocate a home. Please dip in where you will.

The last section is a little more stand-alone. The poems that I write (mostly on my phone during my daily commute) spill out of what is top of my mind. At the time of writing, most days my mother is foremost in my thoughts as she struggles and settles into the nursing care that she needs due to dementia.

This collection is born out of my walk with Jesus in London. I hope you find something that resonates with your life experience or that gives you an honest insight into mine.

Life is great!

Rummaging through my poems, many reflect the joy found in everyday life – the absurd, the exciting and the make-you-pause beauty of it all.

I am repeatedly inspired by the poems of those who have gone before me, by song lyrics and great orators of the past. Equally, some poems are prompted by the passing comments of fellow commuters or a memory that's been nudged awake by a smell or passing sound.

But most of all it's in my daydreams that I find a smile and a line from where a poem grows and blossoms.

Here's a sample.

Warning: limericks included.

I DWELL IN POSSIBILITIES

'I dwell in possibility' - Emily Dickinson

I dwell in the possibilities birthed by the daily Immanuel

I dwell in the possibilities whispered by the wonderful Counsellor

I dwell in the possibilities wrought by the almightiest God

I dwell in the possibilities perpetuated by the everlasting Father

I dwell in the possibilities secured by the Prince of all peace makers

And I dwell with Him where all things have possibilities.

Inspired by Emily Dickinson and
Isaiah 7:14, 9:6 and Mark 10:27.

KNITTED – A PSALM

You created my inmost being; you knitted me together in my mother's womb. I was woven together in the depths of the earth; from the first stitch your eyes saw my unformed body. Before you completed that first row all the days ordained for me were written in your book before one of them came to be.

You selected the yarn by colour, by weight, choosing the texture with utmost care. You picked out the ideal needles, counted the balls of wool and with a smile settled down to cast on that first stitch.

Your fingers blurred into action as you chatted with family, confident of the pattern you yourself designed -

With a knit and a pearl the stitches increased and decreased to ensure the desired shape, maintaining a consistent gauge stitch after stitch, row after row.

And after hours of knitting and chatting, with a satisfied sigh you cast off and held up the result of your handiwork to the light for all to admire.

How precious you are to me. How I wonder at this body knitted together with such love and with such great skill.

I praise you because I am fearfully and wonderfully made.

A riff that was prompted by Psalm 139. I recommend the original.

UNDERSTOOD (ORIGINAL)

His stillent, smally whispers ooze into my mindconscious like a dusk-sweet hotchoc, like a mocha sunrise welcoming wide with embracements louder than fearage, not instructioning, but come in mending, pushing enlightenmentations, praisements and incouragabilities that I inseep onto my naked black and bruises. I tremble-wrap his echo within my born-worn soul but he stainleaks through my weak cardio when I bumpbrush against heartbeatings as fraggi-brittle as mine also. His hushed shade cools and breathes an enveloping: "I understand." And so I restilax in his softly stronging arms.

I overheard some mangled English and noted it down, then added some of my own.

Sometimes we know we're making no sense, but we still need someone to understand.

UNDERSTOOD (REMIX)

His still, small whispers melt into my mind
like hot chocolate at dusk
like a welcoming morning mocha aroma,
with an embrace louder than dawning fears;

Not demanding, but offering healing,
inspiring and revealing –
like a balm to my bruises
like a brace to my body.

And so trembling, I wrap the echo of Him
around my weary soul,
but my weak heart
cannot hold His words
as I bump and brush
against other fragile hearts.

But still I sit in his serene shade
and He breathes these enveloping words:
"I understand."
So I rest in His soft-strong arms.

JOY HAS A NAME

Joy has a name
whispered in awe,
shouted in triumph and
partied abroad.

Joy out-runs
mourning and tears,
drowns out hatred and
drives out fears.

Joy brings peace
and laughter soon after.
Joy gives release and
heals much faster.

Joy has a name
above all others.
His name is Jesus –
joy of many colours.

See Galatians 5:22 for the whole fruit bowl.

Written at Newday, a summer event for teenagers who are open to sun, fun and Jesus.

Sisters

Virgin Vesta perched on the hearth
warming her strong slender hands.
30 years is a very long wait
to have them warmed by a man.
However she knew she could always rely
on the constant warm love of her sisters.
The men could wait while she matured
in sisters' softer caresses.

Vesta was the virgin goddess of the hearth, home, and family in Roman religion. Vestal Virgins pledged celibacy for 30 years.

GHOST IN THE SHELL

Ghost or shell –
be sure it's all me
raising hell

Go see the movie: Ghost in the Shell.

LOVE'S RECEPTION

Her string of choice words rose and fell
wrapping themselves around my eager ears,
like the rise and fall of her pearls
drawing my young eyes,
like the swarm of her subtle scents
filling my brimming heart,
like nothing I had ever heard or seen or felt.
I was captive, she was captor
and oblivious to the spell that held me to her
as she handed my father our room key
and breathed her welcome to Leigh-on-sea.

Love can strike you anywhere, at any age.

STANDING WITH ANGELS

April Fool Phil's in love
and doesn't care what the date is.
What matters is the ring on his finger
that matches his Mrs'.
Standing before their families
gathered from across the miles
beaming smiles toward this happy couple
praying for years of joy
and precious few troubles.

It was the same old song:
their mates were wondering
when they'd get a move on
now their mothers are thinking
of the fruit of the union (don't deny it).
Meanwhile Phil is planning
space for a drum kit
(I wrote that before I saw he'd already unpacked
it)
and Anna is dreaming
of a G&T; and just how Phil is so fit.

So you'll both be forgiven
for failing to notice the party in heaven:
Thousands of angels cheering
with little discretion.
they just love it you see
when plans come to fruition,
when birds of a feather
find such pleasure together.

And they know for sure
the Lord shares their smiles,
cos two of his children
can't help but shine
with the happiness that comes
from deep down knowing
that their love is ordained
by their Father in heaven.

So Phil, so Anna –
we stand with the angels
and shout our congratulations.
We applaud your vows
with more volume
than decorum allows,

-

May the Lord bless you
and keep you,
may his face shine on you
and give you peace
that will never cease
to give you pause to thank Him
for his Grace.

And all the assembled people said:
AMEN

For my good friends Phil and Anna Hamilton, wed on 1 April 2017. What a party!

I'll never forget the look on Anna's face when at the line 'We stand with the angels', the congregation stood and cheered, whooped and applauded for the remainder of the poem, with me shouting over them.

REMEMBER BETTER

Remember to think better,
think further,
think deeper
and with vigour.
Pepper your remember
with colour,
with light,
with friends who delight.
Boost your remember
with story,
with histories,
with cramped group selfies.
And remember your remembers
whenever,
wherever
you drift off centre.
And there you'll discover
your defenders,
your never surrenders
against all contenders.
Then you'll remember
your forevers.

Remember better. It's the best self-defence.

NEW STARTER

Confine your creativity,
limit originality,
dare to be different,
but don't dispute authority.

Blue sky thinking
with a few scattered brainstorms
is no substitution
for you sticking to the norm.

We do value change here
in its right place,
just so long as you ensure
it doesn't leave a trace.

I haven't got to where I am
without these simple laws,
now that's enough chat
let's get on and wash the floors.

Avoid these people. They will hold you back. Product of a poetry class circa 2008.

THE VEGAN KING

The Vegan King
looked across the table
at his son,
wondering where he had gone
so wrong
and what would become
of his kingdom
once he had passed on
his mantle
to a vegetarian.

I misread the title of a novel being read opposite me on the tube: The Vegetarian by Han Kang. I thought it read 'The Vegetarian King'.

You take inspiration where you can find it.

PURPLE RAINBOWS

Deep purple rainbows ground
through my isolation,
their road-show resonating
and shaking my status quo haven.
Singing rivals' swan song,
building a rush-more-strong,
more resilient rock song.
Taking me on to the next page
as I was swept along
and came of age,
relishing my discovery
of a much wider stage
with so much more
than three-chord rage.

As a teenager, I preferred rock. And I still do.

CAPITAL MOVE, SON

If you never try it
you'll never know it,
you'll ever wonder,
forever doubt.
So break out and grab it -
be a chance taker,
a faith placer.
Take the bruises,
absorb the scrapes
that come from escaping safe harbour
and storm the border
of your known neat and orderly
childhood home.
Welcome to London.

I was around 23 years of age, living in the house I'd grown up in, when my father said: "We're moving house."

"Oh, where are we moving to?" I asked.

"No, son, we're moving. It's time you set up on your own."

- *Thanks dad.*

LONDON

I'm a Londoner.
I embrace diversity.
I relish cultural complexity.
I feed on cross border connectivity.
I laugh at the concept of heritage singularity.
I revel in the uncertainty of multi race identity.
I love my God, in His graceful domesticity
here across this broad-shouldered city.

The world has come to London, giving us unasked-for diversity as a gift we did nothing to deserve.

Relish it.

URINAL CHALLENGE

I'm trying to focus
on subtle urinal propriety,
while having to resist
challenges to paternity,
questioning my certainty,
seeding suggestions of penile flaccidity.
And all I want
is to pee with credibility.

Why do motorway service areas post such unsettling adverts about penile dysfunction and paternity tests above the urinals?

FAMILY

There is a young lady named Kay
Who loved to go shopping all day
She'd keep looking around
Until a bargain she found
And no one dared get in her way.

There is a young man named Billy
Who can't help but laugh himself silly
He sniggers and snorts
Guffaws and contorts
Enough to make him feel dizzy.

I'll tell you something about Joe
There's one thing he'll never outgrow
Entertaining his mates
With tales of new scrapes
He'll always put on a great show.

I know a good bloke called Sam
Who has a great number of fans
He won't hesitate
To step up for his mates
And give them a helping hand.

I have a sister named Janet
Who has a wonderful habit
When you need a friend
You can be sure to depend
That she won't get into a panic.

I have a sister named Jenny
Who is always willing and ready
To offer a smile
While cooking with style
I can smell the results already.

I have a sister named Sally
It's hard to keep a clear tally
Of the number of times
She's cheerful and kind
It really makes you feel happy.

HOLLY AND IVY

Holly and Ivy
walked in the woods
discussing who was the best.
Holly was hoping her rosy complexion
would maybe outshine all the rest.

But Ivy thought Holly was surely forgetting
the shock of her prickly demeanour.
She was convinced for sure
the king would adore
all that was so special about her.

Now Ivy was bit of a hugger
you might say a lot of a clinger,
but she was convinced
her warming embrace
would win over the king no matter.

And when the time came
for the winter queen crowning
the king of the woods was clear
he chose as his queen the lady he fell for
and it's Holly who now wears his ring.

As the carol says: "The holly bears the crown."

Prompted by a curious Christmas card featuring two ladies in the snow: Holly and Ivy.

SLOW YOURSELF

Man, slow yourself down,
why you walking so bold?
stridin' like combat,
rushin' to get old.

We'll get there together,
just lift them quick eyes.
Don't miss the already,
reap the realised.

That's how you move,
slide your Kung Fu,
put down your fists
and take a close view.

Come and speak softly,
taste what you knew,
and before you know it
you'll see the true you.

Inspired by various blues tunes. Life is too rich to rush it.

ENABLED

Live out,
live loud,
live strong
and those like you
will laugh in relief
that they are not alone -
that they like you
can be who they were born to be
and can do what they came in this world to do:
Live out loud.

Inspired by a speech by Lord Kelvin Shinkwin and his defence of the disabled – look him up. Those in the womb deserve a voice. Those born with disabilities are not second class citizens.

LORD OF POETRY

Lord, depose our Apollo,
be our true Lord of Poetry
and so give us poetic licence
to fulfil,
to craft,
to create
with a God given palette
in your own imagery.
Blaze a trail from your heart
to the spirits of men,
taking captives and setting them free
to feast on your words of life,
to move to your music of love,
to immerse into an eternity of dance,
to celebrate and so to reflect
your divine Artisan Soul.

Inspired by a passing reference to Apollo. Apparently Apollo was the Olympian god of prophecy and oracles, healing, plague and disease, music, song and poetry, archery, and the protection of the young.

The prevalence of poetry in the Bible tells me that God is the true Lord of Poetry.

Life is tough!

I'm in my mid-fifties. I've been following Jesus' since my mid-teens. In that time I've made plenty of problems for myself through ignorance, error, short-sightedness and plain selfishness. I've also experienced heartache that is none of my own doing.

Following Jesus does not inoculate us from the hardships and challenges of life, but it does give us somewhere to go to help see it through – in the arms of a loving Father. And as I mature and get to know His voice better, I get to avoid pitfalls along the way.

Like the psalmists and others, I have poured my heart out to God when life just doesn't seem fair. And He's been big enough and gracious enough to take the abuse and to listen patiently.

RAIN

The morning rained.
Down in the basement he lay flattened by bad luck and worse judgement.
The morning rained.
Despair seeped under the broken sill as his drained accounts stared back blankly and forecasted worse to come.
The morning rained.
Grey skies cut off the last hint of a silver lining.
The morning rained.
And he cried floods.

Prompted by a scene in a novel – I forget which.

Mud

An early walk with the black dog
can tire the beast.
And for a while
he'll sleep at my feet
and leave me be for another day.

And by evening he'll awake and place
his muddy paw on my knee,
demanding my undivided attention.

Depression is as relentless as a hound.

DOWN

No, not a little down.
Ravaged by a relentless demon
eating at my mind.
Never satisfied,
robbing me for focus,
sapping me of strength
to push back the covers,
never mind the tougher challenges,
like eating and deciding
what to wear.

Maybe tomorrow will be
better,
lighter,
a harbinger of greater hope.

No, not a little down -
a long way further deeper
with a frayed rope
of a hand holding mine
relentless in its determined caress.
God Bless you for being here.

Depression can be a killer – look out for your friends.

SLAP

Why shatter the window with my door wide open?
Why shout with frustration when I'm standing right here?
Why plead so loudly when you have my attention?
Why slap me so hard when I'm wiping your tears?

I see you're so lost, I see you're so lonely,
I feel your hot anger; I feel your deep fears.
Whatever you do, even when you disown me,
I'll sit here beside you, until the fog clears.

Memories of loyalty being tested.

Growing pains

My bones don't fit anymore.
My hair infuriates,
growing wild with rebellion.
My eyes fill at the slightest provocation
while my ears are consumed in flame.
My fingers curl white tight
and my stomach roars with wings
seeking flight.

But my feet continue their reckless shuffle
to a song known only to them
and perhaps to my lips,
but they remain stubbornly dumb.

Memories of adolescence which
seemed to last forever.

SEED

He may have been your father,
but he sure wasn't your daddy.
He may have once donated seed,
but he didn't see it through.

He wasn't there long enough
to be worthy of your affection.
He didn't teach you anything
'cept how to be untrue.

Whatever you feel t'ward him
don't let it redefine you.

The lovely man I see here now
isn't credit to just one screw.

Be your own man. Prompted by a line in a movie: Guardians of the Galaxy.

On the Dance Floor

Next time we meet we'll be dancing.
Callous cancer stole so much,
but not your beauty,
not your love,
not your name written in the Book of Life.

Next time we'll be dancing.
We'll have forgotten our tears,
our anguish,
our defenceless clenched fists
beside the silent plastic bed.

Next time
we'll be too distracted by wonder
to recall any of this.
We'll be too busy dancing.

See you on the dance floor, Lorraine.

In loving memory of Lorraine Purbrick.

Somme

The years stung with gun smoke
and the stench of accusation
hung above the towers of power
as the stark whistles pierced the mourning air.

After a respectful silence,
sodden with sacrifice,
the drizzled grandchildren turned away
for a Starbucked start of a brand new day.

100 years on from the Battle of the Somme, Westminster Square, London, 1 July 2016. It was damp and it was sobering.

PEP TALK

Why so smug?

Seems those pygmy dreams bore fruit long
before you left safe harbour.

Come back home after you have defeated land-
locked fear, hurdled every heaving horizon and
found the stars.

Come back and show me your war torn scars and
deep wild bruises. Show me a worn down ego
and a weathered soul.

And then you can rightly enter eternal harbour
with your head held high.

I recommend a prayer accredited to Sir Francis drake, 'Disturb us, Lord'. You'll find it online. I used that as a starting point for an exercise in a poetry class and ended up with Pep Talk.

THE LAST

His words were leavened with love
as He shared His last mortal meal.
If you listened with care,
His voice maybe cracked with grief
even while His hands were laced with grace
as He broke the crust,
releasing the warmth into the chatter
He shared with His friends.

And if you watched closely,
His hands perhaps shook a little
as He poured out His full bodied wine,
intense in its dark flavour,
infused with fragrance
as if ripe for an altared offering.

And if you looked into His face,
you might have seen a sheen
in the firelight
over the determination to see this through
to the last.

*Jesus didn't have it easy either. This was never more so than at the last meal he had with his friends before his crucifixion. The Last Supper was **tough**.*

Life is easier
with company.

We were not made to fly solo.

I'm grateful for a life-full of friends and family – especially those who have known me the longest and are not afraid to ask the hard questions.

If you've been around me a while, you know that I'm a teary individual (a sensitive child as my school report said). I'm not too big to weep. I appreciate those who let me be myself and love me anyway.

Love you, mate

Love you, mate.
Love your contagious tears
as they breach your ducts,
and gloss your cheeks,
running free and reaching down
past the lump in your throat
to your vulnerable heart.

Love you, mate.
Love your resistance to temptation
to back hand compassion,
emoting with no hesitation,
never embarrassed
to tell the world
that no-one's too big to weep.

You're never too big to weep. Get over it.

Now

If you must breathe -
do it deeply

If you must cry -
do it openly

If you must laugh -
do it heartily

If you must run -
run with me

If you must hide -
hide in me

If you must believe -
believe in me

If you must, and you must,
do so now.

PLAY MATES

Godzilla went walking in the woods
and wondered where Bambi had gone.
He wanted to spend more time with her
for he found her a lovely fun fawn.

He didn't see that last time they met,
when he thought they were having such fun,
his oversized feet weren't that discrete
and Bambi has now been expunged.

Pick your friends carefully.

HUG

A kiss takes a moment
while hugs keep giving
wraparound comfort
and room to weep
cheek to cheek
as a means to keep
skin to skin tenderness,
even in distress
exposing vulnerableness
as we caress,
sighing long and deep
and long and deep
with contented peace,
whispering sweet somethings
and never having to release
and to kiss
goodbye.

Hugs should be available on the NHS.

WHAT'S UP?

You left.
What's up?
Did the WhatsApp offend?
Did we fail to delight?
Or is it just that you're too busy tonight.

We were chatting,
Exchanging,
Goofing,
Emojing.
But all of a sudden
it was clear you were leaving.
(Sad-face-crying.)

- What'sUp?

Social media requires a whole new set of etiquette. Look out for your friends.

HOME FROM HOME

Step over the threshold
and through the front hall
full of shoes and possibilities.
Come to a kitchen table
where you are able
to shed the cold and to unroll your soul
against its worn, warm knots,
flavoured with cookies and coffee mugs
and echoes of late chats and early plans
and sneak-behind hugs.
Let the love that pools here
soak into your marrow,
put aside tomorrow
and so launder your heart clean of fear.
Our home is your home,
come pull up your chair.

I really value the warmth of the homes that welcomed me in as a teenager. I recall the families that made a conscious effort to open their homes and their families to friends of their children. I learned a lot from them about priorities and the importance of nurturing an instinct for inclusion.

This poem is written in acknowledgement of the families who extended their homes to me and my friends. Thank you.

FATHER IS A VERB (EDITED VERSION)

It's not a noun to be worn like some crown.
It's not an honorific.
It's a doing word
beyond what you do with your dick.
It's not some name that you inevitably deserve.
Believe me, fathering is a lifetime of a verb.

Father is something that you ***do****. Even if you have no kids of your own, you can enrich a child's life with a little well placed fathering.*

FATHER IS A VERB (EXTENDED PLAY)

(Let me explain)
Father's Day; and Father Christmas have tried to convince us,
but don't be fooled:
You can, may or will father depending on your mood,
for father is a verb.

It only works in the transitive;
you can't father alone, only in relationship.
It doesn't resent hospital trips,
and offers wrap-around comfort when a partnership splits.

Its touch-line volume drowns out all rivals.
And belly laughs come standard with jokes on recycle.
Yes, father is a verb.

It's something we each do, despite the hour.
It drives right on through the night when life's gone sour.
It'll hammer ten finger nails to get the job done.
It will dance, heedless of decorum, forgetting reputation.

It turns manliness into awesome-men-ness.
It tempers strength with a dose of gentleness,
yes, father is a verb.

Be sure, whoever you are, it works in the singular:
I can father; You can father
(I'm not talking sex here; that takes a partner).
But also, it works in the plural: We can father; and They can father,
Because, you see, in this village it's a joint activity,
we father (and we mother) collaboratively.

It works best in the present tense, happening now not "LATER!"
It can be said in a gentle voice or something - even - quieter;

Sometimes active: directive, protecting;
But often responsive: just sitting,
listening, holding and hugging.
It responds to need you see, but works best proactively, works great sacrificially.
For example, though it cost him dearly, God Fathers us and through us daily.
And one day, suit pressed, He'll proudly walk with the bride of Christ.
And as Father of the bride, He'll host the party and blow the price
(BIGGEST - bar-bill - EVER)
and we'll be sure to save at least one dance for Father.

Oh yes, you heard,
Father is a verb.

BOY IN THE MIDDLE

B-stream Steve looked both ways
longing for what he saw,
thinking he'd be much happier
with those boys he held in awe.

Instead he floundered midstream
never quite feeling satisfied
telling himself that one day soon
he'd climb or slowly slide.

B-stream Steve looked both ways
and found as he got older
the gulfs between a, b and c
were more in the eye of the beholder.

While streaming helped those in charge
he needed to keep in mind
a boy in the middle was much better placed
to befriend those ahead and behind.

Memories of 70's grammar school – and junior school mates in the A and C streams, while I was in the B stream. I really disliked those purple blazers.

Manifesto for an International Church

I believe in one international church.
I believe in an inter-racial and unbiased church of many nations.
I believe in one church of many traditions.
I believe in one church not hemmed in by history or by man-made borders.
I believe in a God for whom his pallet of skin colours reflects his love of diversity.
I believe in God-given racial differences.
I believe in one creator God who made all mankind equal.
I believe in a church that reflects her maker's love of difference.

I do not believe in uniformity.

I believe in the common language of love for one another, for neighbours and for enemies that transcends local dialects.
I believe in one sundry collection of priests who are called to serve one God together, saved by one sacrifice once and for all time.
I believe in the promise of a resurrected church drawn from all generations to meet her bridegroom.
I believe in one eternal wedding feast which features everything from the finest vegetable samosas to the richest steam puddings.

I believe in one extravagant Father who has built one massive mansion with many rooms so all his people can come and dwell together.
I believe – in God's - Kingdom - come.

I worship in a church with 50 plus nationalities represented in its congregation, reflecting the city around it. Diversity is a strength that reflects our Father's heart.

Life is easier with a guide.

The bible is a book of stories about folk like us – some ignorant, some proud, some fearful and some brave, some openhearted, some kind. But all flawed.

We can learn a lot from their stories and from the teaching of Jesus which makes life easier to navigate.

The following poems reflect on passages of the bible that have been a source of guidance for me.

God moves

God of mystery?
I don't think so! --

A God who embraces,
a transformer,
defender,
affirmer,
way-clearer.
Stand by you whatever-er.

A God who endures.
A giver,
a kisser,
a hugger,
commender.
Showing favour no matter-er

A God who comforts.
A deliverer,
protector,
forgiver,
builder-upper-er.
Never put downer.

A God who is proud of you, His followers.
You never need to doubt that He's there for you
Forever-er.

I was reading the letter to the Romans – it was inspiring.

New Levites

We're the New Levites:
The early risers.
The chair setters and cable layers.
We're sound checkers and coffee makers.
We're the greeters, the good to see-yers.
The baby minders, the kids' teachers.
We qualify by turning up,
with willing hands and open hearts.
We're the New Levites and the rota's open.

The Old Testament explains how the priests were drawn from the tribe of Levi. It also explains that the Levites were responsible for a whole host of other roles. The tribe provided treasurers, administrators, artisans, musicians, teachers and even security guards. They kept the whole show on the road. It wasn't all smells and bells in the tribe of Levi.

Nowadays you'll find the New Levites at every church – faithfully serving God's people. Find them and join them.

NOT SO WITH YOU

When tested with power how do you fare?
Does dialogue fade by decree?
When given the chance, does your heart say, "share"
or prompt inadequacy?

Do you run to your fall, pride staining each step?
Or do you season your words with good grace?
Do you pray for each soul you're able to serve?
Or do you treat the whole thing as a race?

Will you grasp for the comfort that comes with position
or like Jesus see it your call
to forfeit self-interest, preferring others,
so to serve them first above all?

This is a riff off a Sunday morning message at Redeemer. How do you handle authority when you are given it? Have a look at Matthew 20: 20-28 to see what Jesus had to say on the matter.

LUNCH BREAK

As I close down, switch off and give you time,
- I hear you.

As I reflect without assumptions, close my lips
and focus on your voice,
- I hear your still, quiet authority over my life.

As I close my eyes to the tears,
- I see with greater clarity who you are.

And I call you:
Most High;
Sovereign Lord;
Eternal God.

As I acknowledge you and accept your provision,
your protection, your prompting,
- I become less and you take your place at the
top of my start up menu.

Dear Father - I am ready to meet with you.

I work at a desk most days. It's easy to eat at my keyboard, rather than logging off and spending some time with my true boss. Follow Jesus' example and take some time alone with your Father. See Matthew 14:23.

THE POET FROM GALILEE

As brave as a poet who knows
that this is too important for prose,
willing to reveal His inner becoming
and patient enough to show
not tell what He's telling,
nor too intent on bringing
the thought down to land,
happy to leave it hovering
leaving us to understand
that the truth is more often
found in the hearing
and not available on demand.
So whoever has ears to hear,
hear this Son of Man.

As I read the gospels it's clear that Jesus didn't spoon feed his followers. He made them think. Sometimes their inability to grasps the lessons he was trying to convey was a source of frustration for Him. But He persisted. You need to listen. See Mark 4.

Inspired by an evening lecture and discussion at St Paul's Cathedral.

NEW FRONT EARS

The new front ears
are eager to hear
all that the Spirit proclaims,
giving a scare
to the old deaf ears
secure in their waxy domains.

The passage is cleared,
good news can be shared
the word of the Father is heard.
It clears the dull heads
of all the misled
with a cry that can't be ignored.

Whoever has ears,
let them each hear
the words of the Son of Man.
They cut like a knife,
but bring you new life.
Come hear the man with the plan.

Sometimes you hear a really bad pun, but you can't ignore it. Thanks go to Joseph Landreth-Smith.

See Mark 4:9 and the surrounding narrative.

NATIVITY SCENE

Stubborn love
faced down the years
of fearful hate
and stared intently as a child
from the stink of a manger
out into the poverty
and the oppression
reflected in captive eyes,
each wide with hope
and wet with joy.

Christmas is all about the miracle of the eternal God becoming a child.

See Isaiah 4:14 and then Matthew 1 and 2.

SPIT

Go empty handed and be fruitful,
lay hands and be liberal
when you pour your oil,
spit in the soil if you have to,
whatever it takes to
bring healing and restoration
to those who have a notion
to listen to you who I have chosen
to bring good news to the nations.
And to each family which shows willing
give greetings
with a voice ringing true
and bringing peace and blessing
to all who reside in their dwelling,
for you are a herald of the most high King
sent to ensure that His shalom and kingdom
hits home before you move on.
Go empty handed and be fruitful,
lay hands and be liberal
when you pour your oil,
spit in the soil if you have to,
Whatever it takes -

Feel the urgency here – go and bless.

See Luke 10 and also John 9:6.

Come to the Table

Come, we have a guest room
where you can recline with your servant king.
He will bathe your sore, dusty feet
and you can rest.

Come commune, join his other friends
and together break bread,
give thanks, sing hymns
and toast his coming kingdom.
Come to the table with honest hearts,
come and in his presence find mercy,
find forgiveness and new purpose.

Come celebrate the covenant
that confers on us a kingdom;
bought by the blood
of the one who came to serve.
Do this in remembrance.
Do this with eagerness.
And when you pray, say:
'Thy Kingdom come.'

Come on! How can you refuse an invitation like that! See Luke 22.

Making waves

Not sinking,
but making waves.

Not the end,
but a brand new start.

Not a dead sacrament,
but a living parable
of the grace of God
of the love of Christ
of the empowering of the Holy Spirit

Not an "I'll try",
but an "I do".

In the name of the Father,
The Son
and the Holy Spirit

AMEN.

It's simple. If you are a believer – go and get yourself baptised.

STUDENT PROPHET

Have I been too revealing
employing too much wailing?
We're the drums a bit too much
with epic trumpets playing?

Have I been too obtuse
or did I veer into rambling?
Could I have better laid it out
without elaborating?

Have I done justice to the discourse?
Did I mis-count the charging horses?
Did I include sufficient angels?
Was I true to my sources?

I trust that I did hold true
to heavenly inspiration,
that the words will stand the test of time
and bring true revelation,

but if I did stray from the truth,
if it all seemed way too bleak,
please respond with good grace -
it's only my first week.

Inspired by wonderings around the Old Testament schools of prophets in training (1 Samuel 19; 2 Kings 2; 2 Kings 4).

21ST CENTURY PROPHET

And the Prophet stood before the people
(in his polo shirt and straight slim jeans)
and spoke (and laughed, and sang)
and shared some of their Father's dreams

"Step out and be unspectacular.
Leave the weird behind.
God selects right royal mess-ups
and then renews their minds

"Think God-thoughts, glimpse your destiny,
but be willing to get it wrong.
Father rewards the risk takers,
not those waiting for perfection.

"The Spirit searches all things
even the deep thoughts of God
and we can grasp what God is saying
because we have the Spirit of God"

With thanks to the teaching of Julian Adams.

1 Corinthians 2:10-16

EVEN THE ENDS

Do you not know?
Have you not heard?
The Lord is the everlasting God,
the creator of the ends of the earth.

Do you not know?
While what you see around you is temporary
While those around you
may not be as dependable
as they might at first seem
there is someone who is never flaky,
someone who does not disappear at the first sign of trouble
(Or, for that matter, at any signs of trouble),
someone who remains when the going gets tough,
someone who stands with you whatever,
someone who goes before you wherever,
someone who is never fazed by what lies around the corner -
because He's been there.

Even if you go to the ends of the earth
He will never grow weary.
His understanding will never be exhausted.
For He created every beginning and every end.
He lasts –
He lasts lifelong.

I recommend the original – go to Isaiah 40

Life is easier with a guide.

Master class.

Jesus said:

"*when* you give…", "*when* you fast…"; "*when* you pray…"

He wasn't giving a beginner's class. He was offering a master class to those already following God. He taught, he coached, he led by example. He showed us how we can excel in giving, in fasting, in praying, in serving God.

The following poems are riffs off a series of teaching at Redeemer London in 2017.

AND WHEN YOU GIVE

And when you give, give like the widow.

And when you give, give til you giggle.

And when you give, give til you've pasted a smile
on every angel within a mile

And when you give, keep them guessing.
Keep it between you and heaven,
cos you know that's better than
a here and now blessing.

Give like the widow,
keep it on the down-low,
but however you chose to give -
just give.

Matthew 6:2-4 and Mark 12: 41-44

AND WHEN YOU FAST

And when you fast, sate your hunger
with more of the Father.

And when you fast, wield it as a weapon
and prepare for battle for his coming kingdom.

And when you fast, fast with intent,
ignore your stomach's dissent
and listen to reflect and listen to expect
more than you had dreamt.

And when you fast, take your fill
of all that he has in store for yours and you.

And whenever you fast, however you fast
don't be downcast, fast with a laugh.

Matthew 6:16-18

AND WHEN YOU PRAY

And when you pray, ask from your heart.

And when you pray, seek from your soul.

And when you pray, sniff around without ceasing.

Look through your tears
to find the doors that he has prepared
to brand new frontiers for His pioneers.

And then –
knock.

Matthew 6:5-15 and 7: 7-12

AND WHEN YOU STAND

And when you stand,
ready to raise your hands in prayer to heaven,
consider your heart and ask –
Do you hold hard feelings?
Anyone who you need to be forgiving?
Any ill feeling that needs divine healing?

Cos if there is
then you know that needs dealing
before you can get to your kneeling
and then your Father can truly hear your appealing.

And don't think it's worth trying concealing.
No, simply deal with it by giving some forgiving
and then you can engage with some honest conversing
with your loving Father listening in heaven.

Mark 11:25

AND WHEN YOU SERVE

And when you serve, start with the feet.
And when you serve, get down low
with a towel and water bowl.

And when you serve, find your honour
not over - but under,
not higher - but lower,
not first - but last.

So when you serve, don't wait your turn,
but push your way to the back
where you'll find nothing to prove,
nothing to hide and nothing to lose,
but your pride.

Yes, you heard;
when you serve, observe his example:
undo a sandal
and start with the feet.

John 13: 1-17 and Matthew 20: 25

AND WHEN YOU READ

And when you read, don't rush –
there’s no need to read with undue speed.

And when you read, start with a suckle –
work up to a nibble until you can gnaw without a dribble.
I encourage you to get down to the marrow like there's no tomorrow.
Savour each word as food for your soul
and live as a model as to how to live whole.

And when you read apply your mind daily,
apply each word liberally (especially to those out of the way, hard to reach places).

And when you read – study.
Sometimes with a buddy, but – study.
This is no hobby; you can't afford to get sloppy.
It's as crucial for the soul as five a day for the body – so study.
And when you read, treat each word like a tutor.
It can teach you how to live shrewder.

And when you read sustain it like a seed,
ensure you pay heed cos it will never mislead.

And when you read do it to a plan,
always with intent and be sure to finish as you began.

And when you read commit to it daily,
commit it to memory to avoid thinking lazily.

And when you read
do it while a commuter, do it on a computer, do it with a kindle, do it with audio, do it with a paperback, do it from front to back.
However you develop the knack, don't let yourself slack.
This Word is no throwback; it will keep you on track.

So just read.

Luke 4. Hebrews 5: 13-14

AND WHEN YOU GIVE (REMIX)

And when you give, give like the widow would,
quietly and thoughtfully, wholeheartedly and consciously
like you know the value of costly,
the value of giving til you laughingly
really hurt in your fund for a holiday.

And when you give keep your other hand
wondering if it's sufficiently,
not knowing if it was sleight of handedly or open handedly
So that you're tempted into giving more than you intended previously.

And when you give, give hilariously
- generously.
Be gutsy til angels agree on the degree
to which you plunge the depths of your kaki's.

And if in doubt just focus on the tree,
on the costly sacrifice He willingly made for you and me.

Give like the widow would - like it's just between you and God –
And set yourself free.

Mum

My mother is in her 80's and over the past year has sunk into the tangle of Vascular Dementia. There are many types of dementia - some creep up on the brain slowly, some don't give much warning. Vascular dementia is the second most common type of dementia and doesn't hang around waiting til you get accustomed to it. In just a few short months Mum has gone from annoying memory loss to being unable to provide for her daily needs and needing nursing care. Watching her deteriorate has felt like watching a friend drowning with no rope to throw to them. Her tears and cries of frustration are something that no one can prepare you for.

I've used pen and paper to vent my anger and keep myself sane. The poems that follow contain the words that I'm able to share. The rest will stay in the drawer.

I'm grateful for my parents' foresight of giving me three great sisters - we give each other support and between us try to tether my mum to her past.

MUUUUM!!

Mum was never happier
than when supping tea with friends,
sharing well-worn wisdom
seen through a mother's lens.

I can't deny I was a teary child
and when mum heard me sobbing
she'd make dash, be there in a flash
and smother me with hugging.

Mum'd appear when needed most,
she had a mother's sonar,
a way of sensing where and when
we would really need her.

Mum had a knack of persuading dad
that it really would be best
to not shout, to let me be
and let me stay half-dressed.

Mum would always find me
when it was time for tea
and it was worth being found by her
not staying an absentee.

Fish fingers at least once a week
followed by arctic roll,
bangers and mash, bubble and squeak.
Don't expect a finger bowl

Mum made each birthday special,
she knew how to stretch the budget.
She'd sit each month with my dad
and work out how to fudge it.

I wouldn't be this man today
if it wasn't for my mum,
her care and warmth, her smile and love
gave me my foundation.

So this mother's day let me say
if your mum is still around
make sure she knows down to her toes
just how much she's loved.

FRAYED

I sit, staring through my tears,
still, against the quiet groaning of a heart
which weeps way beyond my reach,
lost within her fears and aloneness,
only tethered to this world
by a frayed grasp of my hand.

And so I hold on.

LOUDER

Love me a whisper louder,
hold me a squeeze tighter
and kiss me with care.
Tread tenderly
and listen liberally
for right now I need you to lavish wrap-around comfort
and let me fall apart a little more
in your tear stained arms.

TEA LEAVES

Not a brave fight, but a certain defeat.
Not heroic acts, but daily surrender.
Not a close race,
but the frustration of consecutive false starts
and the expectation of an inevitable
expulsion from this life
with no fanfare,
but with a sob and a sigh that sinks like a stone
and pulls her family down around her,
each in stunned silence
engulfed by their memories of lost opportunities,
looking for resolve to do better, somehow.

-

And only, eventually, finding hope in each other
in the shared endeavour to love one another,
together
as she once did a forever ago.

-

Our mother could fill a cup of tea with love like no other.

MISSING

I miss my mother most when I'm in her frenetic company. Such an angry fragile woman in the shadow of the mum she used to be. Lost and alone, wanting a way home - one woman against the world with no old friends, only fresh new foes.

Helpless against every shifting lie and a hundred shifty eyes. Stalkers reprove her, watch her looping moves and corner her as if to prove that we're all conspiring, each trying to rob her - when the screaming truth here is that her fleeting thoughts have already gone where we can never find her - not even in our tears.

MAJESTIC

I aspire for the ambition of a mother:
lifelong and untiring.

Ambition to realise her passion:
providing, serving, loving,
teaching, learning
and persisting all hours with no reflection on reward,
but for the pleasure of the pursuit of her God-given trust -
and so to serve royals and her King with contentment.

And then uniting with Him after a life well lived,
with lives better lived for knowing her.

LASTING GRACE

May the Lord embrace you
and keep you close.

May His kisses rest on your face
and give you assurance of His Grace
that will never cease
to lay down with you
and push away your aloneness.

May His peace increase
until life gives you release
into His everlasting presence.

Amen.

FAMILY RECIPE

(with thanks to my talented sister,
Jenny Marriott)

The strong supportive woman you have always been,
now it's our turn.

The unselfish way you have liberally spread your time on us, right to the edges,
now it's our turn.

The generous helpings of patience that seemed to come so naturally, with seconds for those who want it,
now it's our turn.

Your guiding words seasoned with kindness, so full of flavour,
now it's our turn.

The unconditional love you have always poured out on us, full and overflowing,
now it's our turn...

I just wish you had written down the recipe.

Fin

Thank you for coming. You've been a great audience.

If you still want more, you can find me amongst a world-wide crowd of poets on https://hellopoetry.com

Til next time -

About the Author

My name is Steve Page – welcome to my world.

I'm a poet. There I've said it. I may not look like one to myself when I look in the mirror, but I do write poems, so I must be a poet.

I'm a bloke from London, born and bred. I'm originally from South East London, but I've lived in Ealing, West London, for over 20 years. I worship (pray, sing, cry, hug and shift chairs when needed) at Redeemer Church in Ealing (redeemerlondon.org).

I started my working life as a police officer and later took a left turn through theological college into financial services. I'm now an investigator working in the financial services industry.

While on commute and in my spare time I write poems that reflect my life. I also read a lot of Marvel comic books (which is a whole different form of poetry).

24620163R00075

Printed in Great Britain
by Amazon